If found, please return to:

_____

_____

_____

_____

_____

GRATITUDE

One Line a Day

A THREE-YEAR MEMORY BOOK

CHRONICLE BOOKS
SAN FRANCISCO

ISBN 978-1-7972-0506-9

Manufactured in China.
Design by Kat Yao.
Cover art by Kat Yao.
Typeset in Noyh.

10 9 8 7 6 5 4 3 2 1

Chronicle Books LLC
680 Second Street
San Francisco, California 94107
www.chroniclebooks.com

A condensed, comparative record of your daily gratitude over the course of three years.

HOW TO USE THIS BOOK

To begin, turn to today's calendar date and fill in the year at the top of the page's first entry. Here, you can add your thoughts on the present day's events and all the things for which you are thankful. Do likewise throughout the year. When the year has ended, start the next year in the second entry space on the page, and so on for the remaining entries.

Gratitude is a state of mind, an attitude that you can cultivate.

It's a transformative tool that has powerful effects on your mind, body, and spirit. Studies have shown that a habit of gratitude can improve your health and happiness—it relieves stress, boosts immunity, increases optimism, promotes self-esteem, strengthens relationships, and more. It actually rewires your brain! By combating negative thoughts and focusing on the positive, gratitude creates new neural pathways that change your perception of the world. And best of all, you can access it whenever you want.

Keeping a gratitude journal can help you tap into this resource within yourself. With practice, you will notice more and more things to be thankful for— from memorable experiences and major life events to ordinary moments and little everyday joys. You'll find appreciation for things you may take for granted, like waking up every day or a beautiful sunset. Even challenges and hardships can be seen as opportunities for growth. With time, you will find that every day can be good in some way.

Use this journal to explore your relationship with gratitude. You can write a list of things or one thing in detail. If you find yourself writing the same thing day after day, try being specific. Connect with the emotion; think about why you are grateful for it. You can also record quotes, compliments, or affirmations that resonate with you. There is no right or wrong way. Do whatever works for you. By taking time to focus on what is already good in your life, you'll see the world with more joy and wonder!

Here are some tips to get you started and some questions to get you thinking:

* Slow down, be present, and tune in to the everyday details of your life.

* Sharpen your senses. Pay attention to sight, smell, sound, taste, and touch.

* Observe your surroundings and the natural world around you.

* Think about everything your body does on a daily basis.

* Think about the people in your life. Who helps you? Encourages you? Inspires you?

* Did someone or something make you smile or laugh?

* What qualities or skills are you thankful to have?

* What accomplishments are you proud of?

* What difficulties could be reframed as learning experiences?

* What makes you happy to be alive today?

JANUARY 1

20___ _____
_____
_____
_____
_____
_____

20___ _____
_____
_____
_____
_____
_____

20___ _____
_____
_____
_____
_____
_____

JANUARY 2

20___ _____

_____

_____

_____

_____

_____

20___ _____

_____

_____

_____

_____

_____

20___ _____

_____

_____

_____

_____

_____

JANUARY 3

20___ _____

_____

_____

_____

_____

_____

20___ _____

_____

_____

_____

_____

_____

20___ _____

_____

_____

_____

_____

_____

JANUARY 4

20___ _____
_____
_____
_____
_____
_____

20___ _____
_____
_____
_____
_____
_____

20___ _____
_____
_____
_____
_____
_____

JANUARY 5

20___ _____

_____

_____

_____

_____

_____

20___ _____

_____

_____

_____

_____

_____

20___ _____

_____

_____

_____

_____

_____

JANUARY 6

20___ _____

_____

_____

_____

_____

_____

20___ _____

_____

_____

_____

_____

_____

20___ _____

_____

_____

_____

_____

_____

JANUARY 7

20___ _____

_____

_____

_____

_____

_____

20___ _____

_____

_____

_____

_____

_____

20___ _____

_____

_____

_____

_____

_____

JANUARY 8

20___ _____
_____
_____
_____
_____
_____

20___ _____
_____
_____
_____
_____
_____

20___ _____
_____
_____
_____
_____
_____

JANUARY 9

20___ _____
_____
_____
_____
_____
_____

20___ _____
_____
_____
_____
_____
_____

20___ _____
_____
_____
_____
_____
_____

JANUARY 10

20___ _____

_____

_____

_____

_____

_____

20___ _____

_____

_____

_____

_____

_____

20___ _____

_____

_____

_____

_____

_____

JANUARY 11

20_____ _____

_____

_____

_____

_____

_____

20_____ _____

_____

_____

_____

_____

_____

20_____ _____

_____

_____

_____

_____

_____

JANUARY 12

20___ _____

_____

_____

_____

_____

_____

20___ _____

_____

_____

_____

_____

_____

20___ _____

_____

_____

_____

_____

_____

JANUARY 13

20____ _____

_____

_____

_____

_____

_____

20____ _____

_____

_____

_____

_____

_____

20____ _____

_____

_____

_____

_____

_____

JANUARY 14

20___ _____

_____

_____

_____

_____

_____

20___ _____

_____

_____

_____

_____

_____

20___ _____

_____

_____

_____

_____

_____

JANUARY 15

20___ _____

_____

_____

_____

_____

_____

20___ _____

_____

_____

_____

_____

_____

20___ _____

_____

_____

_____

_____

_____

JANUARY 16

20___ _____

_____

_____

_____

_____

_____

20___ _____

_____

_____

_____

_____

_____

20___ _____

_____

_____

_____

_____

_____

JANUARY 17

20___ _____
_____
_____
_____
_____
_____

20___ _____
_____
_____
_____
_____
_____

20___ _____
_____
_____
_____
_____
_____

JANUARY 18

20___ _____

_____

_____

_____

_____

_____

20___ _____

_____

_____

_____

_____

_____

20___ _____

_____

_____

_____

_____

_____

JANUARY 19

20___ _____

_____

_____

_____

_____

_____

20___ _____

_____

_____

_____

_____

_____

20___ _____

_____

_____

_____

_____

_____

JANUARY 20

20___ _____

_____

_____

_____

_____

_____

20___ _____

_____

_____

_____

_____

_____

20___ _____

_____

_____

_____

_____

_____

JANUARY 21

20___ _____
_____
_____
_____
_____
_____

20___ _____
_____
_____
_____
_____
_____

20___ _____
_____
_____
_____
_____
_____

JANUARY 22

20___ _____

_____

_____

_____

_____

_____

_____

20___ _____

_____

_____

_____

_____

_____

_____

20___ _____

_____

_____

_____

_____

_____

_____

JANUARY 23

20___ _____

_____

_____

_____

_____

_____

20___ _____

_____

_____

_____

_____

_____

20___ _____

_____

_____

_____

_____

_____

JANUARY 24

20___ _____

_____

_____

_____

_____

_____

20___ _____

_____

_____

_____

_____

_____

20___ _____

_____

_____

_____

_____

_____

JANUARY 25

20___ _____

_____

_____

_____

_____

_____

20___ _____

_____

_____

_____

_____

_____

20___ _____

_____

_____

_____

_____

_____

JANUARY 26

20___ _____

_____

_____

_____

_____

_____

20___ _____

_____

_____

_____

_____

_____

20___ _____

_____

_____

_____

_____

_____

JANUARY 27

20___ _____

_____

_____

_____

_____

_____

20___ _____

_____

_____

_____

_____

_____

20___ _____

_____

_____

_____

_____

_____

JANUARY 28

20___ _____

_____

_____

_____

_____

_____

20___ _____

_____

_____

_____

_____

_____

20___ _____

_____

_____

_____

_____

_____

JANUARY 29

20___ _____

_____

_____

_____

_____

_____

20___ _____

_____

_____

_____

_____

_____

20___ _____

_____

_____

_____

_____

_____

JANUARY 30

20___ _____
_____
_____
_____
_____
_____

20___ _____
_____
_____
_____
_____
_____

20___ _____
_____
_____
_____
_____
_____

JANUARY 31

20___ _____

_____

_____

_____

_____

_____

20___ _____

_____

_____

_____

_____

_____

20___ _____

_____

_____

_____

_____

_____

FEBRUARY 1

20___ _____

_____

_____

_____

_____

_____

20___ _____

_____

_____

_____

_____

_____

20___ _____

_____

_____

_____

_____

_____

FEBRUARY 2

20___ _____
_____
_____
_____
_____
_____

20___ _____
_____
_____
_____
_____
_____

20___ _____
_____
_____
_____
_____
_____

FEBRUARY 3

20___ _____

_____

_____

_____

_____

_____

20___ _____

_____

_____

_____

_____

_____

20___ _____

_____

_____

_____

_____

_____

FEBRUARY 4

20___ _____

_____

_____

_____

_____

_____

20___ _____

_____

_____

_____

_____

_____

20___ _____

_____

_____

_____

_____

_____

FEBRUARY 5

20___ _____

_____

_____

_____

_____

_____

20___ _____

_____

_____

_____

_____

_____

20___ _____

_____

_____

_____

_____

_____

FEBRUARY 6

20___ _____

_____

_____

_____

_____

_____

20___ _____

_____

_____

_____

_____

_____

20___ _____

_____

_____

_____

_____

_____

FEBRUARY 7

20___ _____
_____
_____
_____
_____
_____

20___ _____
_____
_____
_____
_____
_____

20___ _____
_____
_____
_____
_____

FEBRUARY 8

20___ _____

_____

_____

_____

_____

_____

20___ _____

_____

_____

_____

_____

_____

20___ _____

_____

_____

_____

_____

_____

FEBRUARY 9

20___ _____

_____

_____

_____

_____

_____

20___ _____

_____

_____

_____

_____

_____

20___ _____

_____

_____

_____

_____

_____

FEBRUARY 10

20___ _____

_____

_____

_____

_____

_____

20___ _____

_____

_____

_____

_____

_____

20___ _____

_____

_____

_____

_____

_____

FEBRUARY 11

20___ _____

_____

_____

_____

_____

_____

20___ _____

_____

_____

_____

_____

_____

20___ _____

_____

_____

_____

_____

_____

FEBRUARY 12

20___ _____

_____

_____

_____

_____

_____

20___ _____

_____

_____

_____

_____

_____

20___ _____

_____

_____

_____

_____

_____

FEBRUARY 13

20___ _____

_____

_____

_____

_____

_____

20___ _____

_____

_____

_____

_____

_____

20___ _____

_____

_____

_____

_____

_____

FEBRUARY 14

20___ _____
_____
_____
_____
_____
_____

20___ _____
_____
_____
_____
_____
_____

20___ _____
_____
_____
_____
_____
_____

FEBRUARY 15

20___ _____

_____

_____

_____

_____

_____

20___ _____

_____

_____

_____

_____

_____

20___ _____

_____

_____

_____

_____

_____

FEBRUARY 16

20___ _____

_____

_____

_____

_____

_____

20___ _____

_____

_____

_____

_____

_____

20___ _____

_____

_____

_____

_____

_____

FEBRUARY 17

20___ _____

_____

_____

_____

_____

_____

20___ _____

_____

_____

_____

_____

_____

20___ _____

_____

_____

_____

_____

_____

FEBRUARY 18

20___ _____
_____
_____
_____
_____
_____

20___ _____
_____
_____
_____
_____
_____

20___ _____
_____
_____
_____
_____
_____

FEBRUARY 19

20___ _____

_____

_____

_____

_____

_____

20___ _____

_____

_____

_____

_____

_____

20___ _____

_____

_____

_____

_____

_____

FEBRUARY 20

20___ _____

_____

_____

_____

_____

_____

20___ _____

_____

_____

_____

_____

_____

20___ _____

_____

_____

_____

_____

_____

FEBRUARY 21

20___ _____

_____

_____

_____

_____

_____

20___ _____

_____

_____

_____

_____

_____

20___ _____

_____

_____

_____

_____

_____

FEBRUARY 22

20___ _____

_____

_____

_____

_____

_____

20___ _____

_____

_____

_____

_____

_____

20___ _____

_____

_____

_____

_____

_____

FEBRUARY 23

20___ _____

_____

_____

_____

_____

_____

20___ _____

_____

_____

_____

_____

_____

20___ _____

_____

_____

_____

_____

_____

FEBRUARY 24

20___ _____

_____

_____

_____

_____

_____

20___ _____

_____

_____

_____

_____

_____

20___ _____

_____

_____

_____

_____

_____

FEBRUARY 25

20____ _____

_____

_____

_____

_____

_____

20____ _____

_____

_____

_____

_____

_____

20____ _____

_____

_____

_____

_____

_____

FEBRUARY 26

20___ _____

_____

_____

_____

_____

_____

20___ _____

_____

_____

_____

_____

_____

20___ _____

_____

_____

_____

_____

_____

FEBRUARY 27

20___ _____

_____

_____

_____

_____

20___ _____

_____

_____

_____

_____

20___ _____

_____

_____

_____

_____

FEBRUARY 28

20___ _____

_____

_____

_____

_____

_____

20___ _____

_____

_____

_____

_____

_____

20___ _____

_____

_____

_____

_____

_____

FEBRUARY 29

20____ _____

_____

_____

_____

_____

_____

20____ _____

_____

_____

_____

_____

_____

20____ _____

_____

_____

_____

_____

_____

MARCH 1

20___ _____

_____

_____

_____

_____

_____

20___ _____

_____

_____

_____

_____

_____

20___ _____

_____

_____

_____

_____

_____

MARCH 2

20___ _____

_____

_____

_____

_____

_____

20___ _____

_____

_____

_____

_____

_____

20___ _____

_____

_____

_____

_____

_____

MARCH 3

20____ _____

_____

_____

_____

_____

_____

20____ _____

_____

_____

_____

_____

_____

20____ _____

_____

_____

_____

_____

_____

MARCH 4

20___ _____

_____

_____

_____

_____

_____

20___ _____

_____

_____

_____

_____

_____

20___ _____

_____

_____

_____

_____

_____

MARCH 5

20_____ _____
_____
_____
_____
_____
_____

20_____ _____
_____
_____
_____
_____
_____

20_____ _____
_____
_____
_____
_____
_____

MARCH 6

20_____ _____

_____

_____

_____

_____

_____

20_____ _____

_____

_____

_____

_____

_____

20_____ _____

_____

_____

_____

_____

_____

MARCH 7

20___ _____

_____

_____

_____

_____

_____

20___ _____

_____

_____

_____

_____

_____

20___ _____

_____

_____

_____

_____

_____

MARCH 8

20___ _____

_____

_____

_____

_____

_____

20___ _____

_____

_____

_____

_____

_____

20___ _____

_____

_____

_____

_____

_____

MARCH 9

20___ _____
_____
_____
_____
_____
_____

20___ _____
_____
_____
_____
_____
_____

20___ _____
_____
_____
_____
_____
_____

MARCH 10

20___ _____

_____

_____

_____

_____

_____

20___ _____

_____

_____

_____

_____

_____

20___ _____

_____

_____

_____

_____

_____

MARCH 11

20___ _____

_____

_____

_____

_____

_____

20___ _____

_____

_____

_____

_____

_____

20___ _____

_____

_____

_____

_____

_____

MARCH 12

20___ _____

_____

_____

_____

_____

_____

20___ _____

_____

_____

_____

_____

_____

20___ _____

_____

_____

_____

_____

_____

MARCH 13

20___ _____
_____
_____
_____
_____
_____

20___ _____
_____
_____
_____
_____
_____

20___ _____
_____
_____
_____
_____
_____

MARCH 14

20___ _____
_____
_____
_____
_____
_____

20___ _____
_____
_____
_____
_____
_____

20___ _____
_____
_____
_____
_____
_____

MARCH 15

20___ _____
_____
_____
_____
_____
_____

20___ _____
_____
_____
_____
_____
_____

20___ _____
_____
_____
_____
_____
_____

MARCH 16

20___ _____

_____

_____

_____

_____

_____

20___ _____

_____

_____

_____

_____

_____

20___ _____

_____

_____

_____

_____

_____

MARCH 17

20___ _____

_____

_____

_____

_____

_____

20___ _____

_____

_____

_____

_____

_____

20___ _____

_____

_____

_____

_____

_____

MARCH 18

20___ _____

_____

_____

_____

_____

_____

20___ _____

_____

_____

_____

_____

_____

20___ _____

_____

_____

_____

_____

_____

MARCH 19

20___ _____

_____

_____

_____

_____

_____

20___ _____

_____

_____

_____

_____

_____

20___ _____

_____

_____

_____

_____

_____

MARCH 20

20___ _____

_____

_____

_____

_____

_____

20___ _____

_____

_____

_____

_____

_____

20___ _____

_____

_____

_____

_____

MARCH 21

20___ _____

_____

_____

_____

_____

_____

20___ _____

_____

_____

_____

_____

_____

20___ _____

_____

_____

_____

_____

_____

MARCH 22

20___ _____

_____

_____

_____

_____

_____

20___ _____

_____

_____

_____

_____

_____

20___ _____

_____

_____

_____

_____

_____

MARCH 23

20___ _____

_____

_____

_____

_____

_____

20___ _____

_____

_____

_____

_____

_____

20___ _____

_____

_____

_____

_____

_____

MARCH 24

20___ _____
_____
_____
_____
_____
_____

20___ _____
_____
_____
_____
_____
_____

20___ _____
_____
_____
_____
_____
_____

MARCH 25

20___ _____

_____

_____

_____

_____

_____

20___ _____

_____

_____

_____

_____

_____

20___ _____

_____

_____

_____

_____

_____

MARCH 26

20___ _____

_____

_____

_____

_____

_____

20___ _____

_____

_____

_____

_____

_____

20___ _____

_____

_____

_____

_____

_____

MARCH 27

20___ _____

_____

_____

_____

_____

_____

20___ _____

_____

_____

_____

_____

_____

20___ _____

_____

_____

_____

_____

_____

MARCH 28

20___ _____

_____

_____

_____

_____

_____

20___ _____

_____

_____

_____

_____

_____

20___ _____

_____

_____

_____

_____

_____

MARCH 29

20___ _____

_____

_____

_____

_____

_____

20___ _____

_____

_____

_____

_____

_____

20___ _____

_____

_____

_____

_____

_____

MARCH 30

20___ _____

20___ _____

20___ _____

MARCH 31

20___ _____

_____

_____

_____

_____

_____

20___ _____

_____

_____

_____

_____

_____

20___ _____

_____

_____

_____

_____

_____

APRIL 1

20___ _____

_____

_____

_____

_____

_____

20___ _____

_____

_____

_____

_____

_____

20___ _____

_____

_____

_____

_____

_____

APRIL 2

20___ _____

_____

_____

_____

_____

_____

20___ _____

_____

_____

_____

_____

_____

20___ _____

_____

_____

_____

_____

_____

APRIL 3

20___ _____

_____

_____

_____

_____

_____

20___ _____

_____

_____

_____

_____

_____

20___ _____

_____

_____

_____

_____

_____

APRIL 4

20___ _____
_____
_____
_____
_____
_____

20___ _____
_____
_____
_____
_____
_____

20___ _____
_____
_____
_____
_____
_____

APRIL 5

20___ _____

_____

_____

_____

_____

_____

20___ _____

_____

_____

_____

_____

_____

20___ _____

_____

_____

_____

_____

_____

APRIL 6

20___ _____

_____

_____

_____

_____

_____

20___ _____

_____

_____

_____

_____

_____

20___ _____

_____

_____

_____

_____

_____

APRIL 7

20____ _____

_____

_____

_____

_____

_____

20____ _____

_____

_____

_____

_____

_____

20____ _____

_____

_____

_____

_____

_____

APRIL 8

20___ _____
_____
_____
_____
_____
_____

20___ _____
_____
_____
_____
_____
_____

20___ _____
_____
_____
_____
_____
_____

APRIL 9

20___ _____

_____

_____

_____

_____

_____

20___ _____

_____

_____

_____

_____

_____

20___ _____

_____

_____

_____

_____

_____

APRIL 10

20___ _____

_____

_____

_____

_____

_____

20___ _____

_____

_____

_____

_____

_____

20___ _____

_____

_____

_____

_____

_____

APRIL 11

20___ _____

_____

_____

_____

_____

_____

20___ _____

_____

_____

_____

_____

_____

20___ _____

_____

_____

_____

_____

_____

APRIL 12

20____ _____

_____

_____

_____

_____

_____

20____ _____

_____

_____

_____

_____

_____

20____ _____

_____

_____

_____

_____

_____

APRIL 13

20___ _____

_____

_____

_____

_____

_____

20___ _____

_____

_____

_____

_____

_____

20___ _____

_____

_____

_____

_____

_____

APRIL 14

20___ _____

_____

_____

_____

_____

_____

20___ _____

_____

_____

_____

_____

_____

20___ _____

_____

_____

_____

_____

_____

APRIL 15

20___ _____

_____

_____

_____

_____

_____

20___ _____

_____

_____

_____

_____

_____

20___ _____

_____

_____

_____

_____

_____

APRIL 16

20____ _____
_____
_____
_____
_____
_____

20____ _____
_____
_____
_____
_____
_____

20____ _____
_____
_____
_____
_____
_____

APRIL 17

20___ _____

_____

_____

_____

_____

_____

_____

20___ _____

_____

_____

_____

_____

_____

_____

20___ _____

_____

_____

_____

_____

_____

_____

APRIL 18

20___ _____
_____
_____
_____
_____
_____

20___ _____
_____
_____
_____
_____
_____

20___ _____
_____
_____
_____
_____
_____

APRIL 19

20___ _____

_____

_____

_____

_____

_____

20___ _____

_____

_____

_____

_____

_____

20___ _____

_____

_____

_____

_____

_____

APRIL 20

20___ _____

_____

_____

_____

_____

_____

20___ _____

_____

_____

_____

_____

_____

20___ _____

_____

_____

_____

_____

_____

APRIL 21

20___ _____

_____

_____

_____

_____

_____

20___ _____

_____

_____

_____

_____

_____

20___ _____

_____

_____

_____

_____

_____

APRIL 22

20___ _____

_____

_____

_____

_____

_____

20___ _____

_____

_____

_____

_____

_____

20___ _____

_____

_____

_____

_____

_____

APRIL 23

20___ _____

_____

_____

_____

_____

_____

20___ _____

_____

_____

_____

_____

_____

20___ _____

_____

_____

_____

_____

_____

APRIL 24

20___ _____
_____
_____
_____
_____
_____

20___ _____
_____
_____
_____
_____
_____

20___ _____
_____
_____
_____
_____
_____

APRIL 25

20____ _____

_____

_____

_____

_____

_____

20____ _____

_____

_____

_____

_____

_____

20____ _____

_____

_____

_____

_____

_____

APRIL 26

20___ _____

_____

_____

_____

_____

20___ _____

_____

_____

_____

_____

20___ _____

_____

_____

_____

_____

APRIL 27

20___ _____

_____

_____

_____

_____

_____

20___ _____

_____

_____

_____

_____

_____

20___ _____

_____

_____

_____

_____

_____

APRIL 28

20___ _____

20___ _____

20___ _____

APRIL 29

20___ _____

_____

_____

_____

_____

_____

20___ _____

_____

_____

_____

_____

_____

20___ _____

_____

_____

_____

_____

_____

APRIL 30

20___ _____

20___ _____

20___ _____

MAY 1

20___ _____

_____

_____

_____

_____

_____

20___ _____

_____

_____

_____

_____

_____

20___ _____

_____

_____

_____

_____

_____

MAY 2

20___ _____

_____

_____

_____

_____

_____

20___ _____

_____

_____

_____

_____

_____

20___ _____

_____

_____

_____

_____

_____

MAY 3

20___ _____
_____
_____
_____
_____
_____

20___ _____
_____
_____
_____
_____
_____

20___ _____
_____
_____
_____
_____
_____

MAY 4

20___ _____

_____

_____

_____

_____

_____

20___ _____

_____

_____

_____

_____

_____

20___ _____

_____

_____

_____

_____

_____

MAY 5

20___ _____

_____

_____

_____

_____

_____

20___ _____

_____

_____

_____

_____

_____

20___ _____

_____

_____

_____

_____

_____

MAY 6

20___ _____

_____

_____

_____

_____

_____

20___ _____

_____

_____

_____

_____

_____

20___ _____

_____

_____

_____

_____

_____

MAY 7

20___ _____

_____

_____

_____

_____

_____

20___ _____

_____

_____

_____

_____

_____

20___ _____

_____

_____

_____

_____

_____

MAY 8

20___ _____
_____
_____
_____
_____
_____

20___ _____
_____
_____
_____
_____
_____

20___ _____
_____
_____
_____
_____
_____

MAY 9

20___ _____

_____

_____

_____

_____

_____

20___ _____

_____

_____

_____

_____

_____

20___ _____

_____

_____

_____

_____

_____

MAY 10

20___ _____

_____

_____

_____

_____

_____

20___ _____

_____

_____

_____

_____

_____

20___ _____

_____

_____

_____

_____

_____

MAY 11

20___ _____

_____

_____

_____

_____

_____

20___ _____

_____

_____

_____

_____

_____

20___ _____

_____

_____

_____

_____

_____

MAY 12

20___ _____

20___ _____

20___ _____

MAY 13

20___ _____

_____

_____

_____

_____

_____

20___ _____

_____

_____

_____

_____

_____

20___ _____

_____

_____

_____

_____

_____

MAY 14

20___ _____

_____

_____

_____

_____

_____

20___ _____

_____

_____

_____

_____

_____

20___ _____

_____

_____

_____

_____

_____

MAY 15

20___ _____

_____

_____

_____

_____

_____

20___ _____

_____

_____

_____

_____

_____

20___ _____

_____

_____

_____

_____

_____

MAY 16

20___ _____

_____

_____

_____

_____

_____

20___ _____

_____

_____

_____

_____

_____

20___ _____

_____

_____

_____

_____

_____

MAY 17

20___ _____

20___ _____

20___ _____

MAY 18

20___ _____

_____

_____

_____

_____

_____

20___ _____

_____

_____

_____

_____

_____

20___ _____

_____

_____

_____

_____

_____

MAY 19

20___ _____

_____

_____

_____

_____

_____

20___ _____

_____

_____

_____

_____

_____

20___ _____

_____

_____

_____

_____

_____

MAY 20

20___ _____

_____

_____

_____

_____

_____

20___ _____

_____

_____

_____

_____

_____

20___ _____

_____

_____

_____

_____

_____

MAY 21

20___ _____

_____

_____

_____

_____

_____

20___ _____

_____

_____

_____

_____

_____

20___ _____

_____

_____

_____

_____

_____

MAY 22

20___ _____

_____

_____

_____

_____

_____

20___ _____

_____

_____

_____

_____

_____

20___ _____

_____

_____

_____

_____

_____

MAY 23

20___ _____

_____

_____

_____

_____

_____

20___ _____

_____

_____

_____

_____

_____

20___ _____

_____

_____

_____

_____

_____

MAY 24

20___ _____

20___ _____

20___ _____

MAY 25

20___ _____

_____

_____

_____

_____

_____

20___ _____

_____

_____

_____

_____

_____

20___ _____

_____

_____

_____

_____

_____

MAY 26

20___ _____
_____
_____
_____
_____
_____

20___ _____
_____
_____
_____
_____
_____

20___ _____
_____
_____
_____
_____
_____

MAY 27

20___ _____

_____

_____

_____

_____

_____

20___ _____

_____

_____

_____

_____

_____

20___ _____

_____

_____

_____

_____

_____

MAY 28

20___ _____
_____
_____
_____
_____
_____

20___ _____
_____
_____
_____
_____
_____

20___ _____
_____
_____
_____
_____
_____

MAY 29

20____ _____

_____

_____

_____

_____

_____

20____ _____

_____

_____

_____

_____

_____

20____ _____

_____

_____

_____

_____

_____

MAY 30

20___ _____

_____

_____

_____

_____

_____

20___ _____

_____

_____

_____

_____

_____

20___ _____

_____

_____

_____

_____

_____

_____

MAY 31

20___ _____
_____
_____
_____
_____
_____

20___ _____
_____
_____
_____
_____
_____

20___ _____
_____
_____
_____
_____
_____

JUNE 1

20___ _____

_____

_____

_____

_____

_____

20___ _____

_____

_____

_____

_____

_____

20___ _____

_____

_____

_____

_____

_____

JUNE 2

20___ _____
_____
_____
_____
_____
_____

20___ _____
_____
_____
_____
_____
_____

20___ _____
_____
_____
_____
_____
_____

JUNE 3

20___ _____
_____
_____
_____
_____
_____

20___ _____
_____
_____
_____
_____
_____

20___ _____
_____
_____
_____
_____
_____

JUNE 4

20___ _____

_____

_____

_____

_____

_____

20___ _____

_____

_____

_____

_____

_____

20___ _____

_____

_____

_____

_____

_____

JUNE 5

20___ _____
_____
_____
_____
_____
_____

20___ _____
_____
_____
_____
_____
_____

20___ _____
_____
_____
_____
_____
_____

JUNE 6

20___ _____

_____

_____

_____

_____

_____

20___ _____

_____

_____

_____

_____

_____

20___ _____

_____

_____

_____

_____

_____

JUNE 7

20___ _____
_____
_____
_____
_____
_____

20___ _____
_____
_____
_____
_____
_____

20___ _____
_____
_____
_____
_____
_____

JUNE 8

20___ _____

_____

_____

_____

_____

_____

20___ _____

_____

_____

_____

_____

_____

20___ _____

_____

_____

_____

_____

_____

JUNE 9

20___ _____

_____

_____

_____

_____

_____

20___ _____

_____

_____

_____

_____

_____

20___ _____

_____

_____

_____

_____

_____

JUNE 10

20___ _____

_____

_____

_____

_____

_____

20___ _____

_____

_____

_____

_____

_____

20___ _____

_____

_____

_____

_____

_____

JUNE 11

20___ _____

_____

_____

_____

_____

_____

20___ _____

_____

_____

_____

_____

_____

20___ _____

_____

_____

_____

_____

_____

JUNE 12

20___ _____

_____

_____

_____

_____

_____

20___ _____

_____

_____

_____

_____

_____

20___ _____

_____

_____

_____

_____

_____

JUNE 13

20___ _____

_____

_____

_____

_____

_____

20___ _____

_____

_____

_____

_____

_____

20___ _____

_____

_____

_____

_____

_____

JUNE 14

20___ _____

_____

_____

_____

_____

_____

20___ _____

_____

_____

_____

_____

_____

20___ _____

_____

_____

_____

_____

_____

JUNE 15

20___ _____

_____

_____

_____

_____

_____

20___ _____

_____

_____

_____

_____

_____

20___ _____

_____

_____

_____

_____

_____

JUNE 16

20___ _____
_____
_____
_____
_____
_____

20___ _____
_____
_____
_____
_____
_____

20___ _____
_____
_____
_____
_____
_____

JUNE 17

20___ _____

_____

_____

_____

_____

_____

20___ _____

_____

_____

_____

_____

_____

20___ _____

_____

_____

_____

_____

_____

JUNE 18

20___ _____

_____

_____

_____

_____

_____

20___ _____

_____

_____

_____

_____

_____

20___ _____

_____

_____

_____

_____

_____

JUNE 19

20___ _____

_____

_____

_____

_____

_____

20___ _____

_____

_____

_____

_____

_____

20___ _____

_____

_____

_____

_____

_____

JUNE 20

20___ _____

_____

_____

_____

_____

_____

20___ _____

_____

_____

_____

_____

_____

20___ _____

_____

_____

_____

_____

_____

JUNE 21

20___ _____

_____

_____

_____

_____

_____

20___ _____

_____

_____

_____

_____

_____

20___ _____

_____

_____

_____

_____

_____

JUNE 22

20___ _____

_____

_____

_____

_____

_____

20___ _____

_____

_____

_____

_____

_____

20___ _____

_____

_____

_____

_____

_____

JUNE 23

20____ _____

_____

_____

_____

_____

_____

20____ _____

_____

_____

_____

_____

_____

20____ _____

_____

_____

_____

_____

_____

JUNE 24

20___ _____

_____

_____

_____

_____

_____

20___ _____

_____

_____

_____

_____

_____

20___ _____

_____

_____

_____

_____

_____

JUNE 25

20___ _____
_____
_____
_____
_____
_____

20___ _____
_____
_____
_____
_____
_____

20___ _____
_____
_____
_____
_____
_____

JUNE 26

20___ _____

_____

_____

_____

_____

_____

20___ _____

_____

_____

_____

_____

_____

20___ _____

_____

_____

_____

_____

_____

JUNE 27

20___ _____

20___ _____

20___ _____

JUNE 28

20___ _____

_____

_____

_____

_____

_____

20___ _____

_____

_____

_____

_____

_____

20___ _____

_____

_____

_____

_____

_____

JUNE 29

20___ _____

_____

_____

_____

_____

_____

20___ _____

_____

_____

_____

_____

_____

20___ _____

_____

_____

_____

_____

_____

JUNE 30

20___ _____

_____

_____

_____

_____

_____

20___ _____

_____

_____

_____

_____

_____

20___ _____

_____

_____

_____

_____

_____

JULY 1

20___ _____

_____

_____

_____

_____

_____

20___ _____

_____

_____

_____

_____

_____

20___ _____

_____

_____

_____

_____

_____

JULY 2

20___ _____

_____

_____

_____

_____

_____

20___ _____

_____

_____

_____

_____

_____

20___ _____

_____

_____

_____

_____

_____

JULY 3

20___ _____

_____

_____

_____

_____

_____

20___ _____

_____

_____

_____

_____

_____

20___ _____

_____

_____

_____

_____

_____

JULY 4

20___ _____

_____

_____

_____

_____

_____

20___ _____

_____

_____

_____

_____

_____

20___ _____

_____

_____

_____

_____

_____

JULY 5

20___ _____

_____

_____

_____

_____

_____

20___ _____

_____

_____

_____

_____

_____

20___ _____

_____

_____

_____

_____

_____

JULY 6

20___ _____

_____

_____

_____

_____

_____

20___ _____

_____

_____

_____

_____

_____

20___ _____

_____

_____

_____

_____

_____

JULY 7

20___ _____

_____

_____

_____

_____

_____

20___ _____

_____

_____

_____

_____

_____

20___ _____

_____

_____

_____

_____

_____

JULY 8

20___ _____

_____

_____

_____

_____

_____

20___ _____

_____

_____

_____

_____

_____

20___ _____

_____

_____

_____

_____

_____

JULY 9

20___ _____

_____

_____

_____

_____

_____

20___ _____

_____

_____

_____

_____

_____

20___ _____

_____

_____

_____

_____

_____

JULY 10

20___ _____

_____

_____

_____

_____

_____

20___ _____

_____

_____

_____

_____

_____

20___ _____

_____

_____

_____

_____

_____

JULY 11

20___ _____
_____
_____
_____
_____
_____

20___ _____
_____
_____
_____
_____
_____

20___ _____
_____
_____
_____
_____
_____

JULY 12

20___ _____

_____

_____

_____

_____

_____

_____

20___ _____

_____

_____

_____

_____

_____

_____

20___ _____

_____

_____

_____

_____

_____

JULY 13

20___ _____

_____

_____

_____

_____

_____

20___ _____

_____

_____

_____

_____

_____

20___ _____

_____

_____

_____

_____

_____

JULY 14

20___ _____

_____

_____

_____

_____

_____

20___ _____

_____

_____

_____

_____

_____

20___ _____

_____

_____

_____

_____

_____

JULY 15

20___ _____
_____
_____
_____
_____
_____

20___ _____
_____
_____
_____
_____
_____

20___ _____
_____
_____
_____
_____
_____

JULY 16

20___ _____
_____
_____
_____
_____
_____

20___ _____
_____
_____
_____
_____
_____

20___ _____
_____
_____
_____
_____
_____

JULY 17

20___ _____
_____
_____
_____
_____
_____

20___ _____
_____
_____
_____
_____
_____

20___ _____
_____
_____
_____
_____
_____

JULY 18

20___ _____

_____

_____

_____

_____

_____

20___ _____

_____

_____

_____

_____

_____

20___ _____

_____

_____

_____

_____

_____

JULY 19

20___ _____

_____

_____

_____

_____

_____

20___ _____

_____

_____

_____

_____

_____

20___ _____

_____

_____

_____

_____

_____

JULY 20

20___ _____

_____

_____

_____

_____

_____

20___ _____

_____

_____

_____

_____

_____

20___ _____

_____

_____

_____

_____

_____

JULY 21

20___ _____
_____
_____
_____
_____
_____

20___ _____
_____
_____
_____
_____
_____

20___ _____
_____
_____
_____
_____
_____

JULY 22

20___ _____

_____

_____

_____

_____

_____

20___ _____

_____

_____

_____

_____

_____

20___ _____

_____

_____

_____

_____

_____

JULY 23

20___ _____
_____
_____
_____
_____
_____

20___ _____
_____
_____
_____
_____
_____

20___ _____
_____
_____
_____
_____
_____

JULY 24

20___ _____

_____

_____

_____

_____

_____

20___ _____

_____

_____

_____

_____

_____

20___ _____

_____

_____

_____

_____

_____

JULY 25

20___ _____

_____

_____

_____

_____

_____

20___ _____

_____

_____

_____

_____

_____

20___ _____

_____

_____

_____

_____

_____

JULY 26

20___ _____

_____

_____

_____

_____

_____

20___ _____

_____

_____

_____

_____

_____

20___ _____

_____

_____

_____

_____

_____

JULY 27

20___ _____
_____
_____
_____
_____
_____

20___ _____
_____
_____
_____
_____
_____

20___ _____
_____
_____
_____
_____
_____

JULY 28

20___ _____
_____
_____
_____
_____
_____

20___ _____
_____
_____
_____
_____
_____

20___ _____
_____
_____
_____
_____
_____

JULY 29

20___ _____

20___ _____

20___ _____

JULY 30

20___ _____

_____

_____

_____

_____

_____

20___ _____

_____

_____

_____

_____

_____

20___ _____

_____

_____

_____

_____

_____

JULY 31

20____ _____

20____ _____

20____ _____

AUGUST 1

20___ _____

_____

_____

_____

_____

_____

20___ _____

_____

_____

_____

_____

_____

20___ _____

_____

_____

_____

_____

_____

AUGUST 2

20___ _____

_____

_____

_____

_____

_____

20___ _____

_____

_____

_____

_____

_____

20___ _____

_____

_____

_____

_____

_____

AUGUST 3

20___ _____

_____

_____

_____

_____

20___ _____

_____

_____

_____

_____

20___ _____

_____

_____

_____

_____

AUGUST 4

20___ _____

_____

_____

_____

_____

_____

20___ _____

_____

_____

_____

_____

_____

20___ _____

_____

_____

_____

_____

_____

AUGUST 5

20___ _____

_____

_____

_____

_____

_____

20___ _____

_____

_____

_____

_____

_____

20___ _____

_____

_____

_____

_____

_____

AUGUST 6

20___ _____

_____

_____

_____

_____

_____

20___ _____

_____

_____

_____

_____

_____

20___ _____

_____

_____

_____

_____

_____

AUGUST 7

20___ _____

_____

_____

_____

_____

_____

20___ _____

_____

_____

_____

_____

_____

20___ _____

_____

_____

_____

_____

_____

AUGUST 8

20___ _____
_____
_____
_____
_____
_____

20___ _____
_____
_____
_____
_____
_____

20___ _____
_____
_____
_____
_____
_____

AUGUST 9

20___ _____

_____

_____

_____

_____

_____

20___ _____

_____

_____

_____

_____

_____

20___ _____

_____

_____

_____

_____

_____

AUGUST 10

20___ _____

_____

_____

_____

_____

_____

20___ _____

_____

_____

_____

_____

_____

20___ _____

_____

_____

_____

_____

_____

AUGUST 11

20___ _____

_____

_____

_____

_____

_____

20___ _____

_____

_____

_____

_____

_____

20___ _____

_____

_____

_____

_____

_____

AUGUST 12

20___ _____
_____
_____
_____
_____
_____

20___ _____
_____
_____
_____
_____
_____

20___ _____
_____
_____
_____
_____
_____

AUGUST 13

20___ _____

_____

_____

_____

_____

_____

20___ _____

_____

_____

_____

_____

_____

20___ _____

_____

_____

_____

_____

_____

AUGUST 14

20___ _____
_____
_____
_____
_____
_____

20___ _____
_____
_____
_____
_____
_____

20___ _____
_____
_____
_____
_____
_____

AUGUST 15

20___ _____

_____

_____

_____

_____

_____

20___ _____

_____

_____

_____

_____

_____

20___ _____

_____

_____

_____

_____

_____

AUGUST 16

20___ _____
_____
_____
_____
_____
_____

20___ _____
_____
_____
_____
_____
_____

20___ _____
_____
_____
_____
_____
_____

AUGUST 17

20___ _____

_____

_____

_____

_____

_____

20___ _____

_____

_____

_____

_____

_____

20___ _____

_____

_____

_____

_____

_____

AUGUST 18

20___ _____

_____

_____

_____

_____

_____

20___ _____

_____

_____

_____

_____

_____

20___ _____

_____

_____

_____

_____

AUGUST 19

20___ _____

_____

_____

_____

_____

_____

20___ _____

_____

_____

_____

_____

_____

20___ _____

_____

_____

_____

_____

_____

AUGUST 20

20___ _____

_____

_____

_____

_____

_____

20___ _____

_____

_____

_____

_____

_____

20___ _____

_____

_____

_____

_____

_____

AUGUST 21

20___ _____

_____

_____

_____

_____

_____

20___ _____

_____

_____

_____

_____

_____

20___ _____

_____

_____

_____

_____

_____

AUGUST 22

20___ _____
_____
_____
_____
_____
_____

20___ _____
_____
_____
_____
_____
_____

20___ _____
_____
_____
_____
_____
_____

AUGUST 23

20___ _____

_____

_____

_____

_____

_____

20___ _____

_____

_____

_____

_____

_____

20___ _____

_____

_____

_____

_____

_____

AUGUST 24

20___ _____

_____

_____

_____

_____

_____

20___ _____

_____

_____

_____

_____

_____

20___ _____

_____

_____

_____

_____

_____

AUGUST 25

20___ _____
_____
_____
_____
_____
_____

20___ _____
_____
_____
_____
_____
_____

20___ _____
_____
_____
_____
_____
_____

AUGUST 26

20___ _____

_____

_____

_____

_____

_____

20___ _____

_____

_____

_____

_____

_____

20___ _____

_____

_____

_____

_____

_____

AUGUST 27

20___ _____

_____

_____

_____

_____

_____

20___ _____

_____

_____

_____

_____

_____

20___ _____

_____

_____

_____

_____

_____

AUGUST 28

20___ _____

_____

_____

_____

_____

_____

20___ _____

_____

_____

_____

_____

_____

20___ _____

_____

_____

_____

_____

_____

AUGUST 29

20___ _____

_____

_____

_____

_____

_____

20___ _____

_____

_____

_____

_____

_____

20___ _____

_____

_____

_____

_____

_____

AUGUST 30

20___ _____
_____
_____
_____
_____
_____

20___ _____
_____
_____
_____
_____
_____

20___ _____
_____
_____
_____
_____
_____

AUGUST 31

20_____ _____
_____
_____
_____
_____
_____

20_____ _____
_____
_____
_____
_____
_____

20_____ _____
_____
_____
_____
_____
_____

SEPTEMBER 1

20___ _____

_____

_____

_____

_____

20___ _____

_____

_____

_____

_____

20___ _____

_____

_____

_____

_____

SEPTEMBER 2

20___ _____

_____

_____

_____

_____

_____

20___ _____

_____

_____

_____

_____

_____

20___ _____

_____

_____

_____

_____

_____

SEPTEMBER 3

20___ _____
_____
_____
_____
_____
_____

20___ _____
_____
_____
_____
_____
_____

20___ _____
_____
_____
_____
_____
_____

SEPTEMBER 4

20___ _____

_____

_____

_____

_____

_____

20___ _____

_____

_____

_____

_____

_____

20___ _____

_____

_____

_____

_____

_____

SEPTEMBER 5

20___ _____

_____

_____

_____

_____

_____

20___ _____

_____

_____

_____

_____

_____

20___ _____

_____

_____

_____

_____

_____

SEPTEMBER 6

20___ _____

_____

_____

_____

_____

_____

20___ _____

_____

_____

_____

_____

_____

20___ _____

_____

_____

_____

_____

_____

SEPTEMBER 7

20___ _____

_____

_____

_____

_____

_____

20___ _____

_____

_____

_____

_____

_____

20___ _____

_____

_____

_____

_____

_____

SEPTEMBER 8

20___ _____

_____

_____

_____

_____

_____

20___ _____

_____

_____

_____

_____

_____

20___ _____

_____

_____

_____

_____

_____

SEPTEMBER 9

20___ _____

_____

_____

_____

_____

_____

20___ _____

_____

_____

_____

_____

_____

20___ _____

_____

_____

_____

_____

_____

SEPTEMBER 10

20___ _____

_____

_____

_____

_____

_____

20___ _____

_____

_____

_____

_____

_____

20___ _____

_____

_____

_____

_____

_____

SEPTEMBER 11

20___ _____

_____

_____

_____

_____

_____

20___ _____

_____

_____

_____

_____

_____

20___ _____

_____

_____

_____

_____

_____

_____

SEPTEMBER 12

20___ _____

_____

_____

_____

_____

_____

20___ _____

_____

_____

_____

_____

_____

20___ _____

_____

_____

_____

_____

_____

SEPTEMBER 13

20___ _____

_____

_____

_____

_____

_____

20___ _____

_____

_____

_____

_____

_____

20___ _____

_____

_____

_____

_____

_____

SEPTEMBER 14

20___ _____

20___ _____

20___ _____

SEPTEMBER 15

20___ _____

_____

_____

_____

_____

_____

20___ _____

_____

_____

_____

_____

_____

20___ _____

_____

_____

_____

_____

_____

SEPTEMBER 16

20___ _____

_____

_____

_____

_____

_____

20___ _____

_____

_____

_____

_____

_____

20___ _____

_____

_____

_____

_____

_____

SEPTEMBER 17

20___ _____

_____

_____

_____

_____

_____

20___ _____

_____

_____

_____

_____

_____

20___ _____

_____

_____

_____

_____

_____

SEPTEMBER 18

20___ _____

_____

_____

_____

_____

_____

20___ _____

_____

_____

_____

_____

_____

20___ _____

_____

_____

_____

_____

_____

SEPTEMBER 19

20___ _____
_____
_____
_____
_____
_____

20___ _____
_____
_____
_____
_____
_____

20___ _____
_____
_____
_____
_____
_____

SEPTEMBER 20

20___ _____

_____

_____

_____

_____

_____

20___ _____

_____

_____

_____

_____

_____

20___ _____

_____

_____

_____

_____

_____

SEPTEMBER 21

20___ _____

_____

_____

_____

_____

_____

20___ _____

_____

_____

_____

_____

_____

20___ _____

_____

_____

_____

_____

_____

SEPTEMBER 22

20___ _____

_____

_____

_____

_____

_____

20___ _____

_____

_____

_____

_____

_____

20___ _____

_____

_____

_____

_____

_____

SEPTEMBER 23

20___ _____

_____

_____

_____

_____

_____

20___ _____

_____

_____

_____

_____

_____

20___ _____

_____

_____

_____

_____

_____

SEPTEMBER 24

20___ _____

_____

_____

_____

_____

_____

20___ _____

_____

_____

_____

_____

_____

20___ _____

_____

_____

_____

_____

_____

SEPTEMBER 25

20___ _____

_____

_____

_____

_____

_____

20___ _____

_____

_____

_____

_____

_____

20___ _____

_____

_____

_____

_____

_____

SEPTEMBER 26

20___ _____

_____

_____

_____

_____

_____

20___ _____

_____

_____

_____

_____

_____

20___ _____

_____

_____

_____

_____

_____

SEPTEMBER 27

20___ _____

_____

_____

_____

_____

_____

20___ _____

_____

_____

_____

_____

_____

20___ _____

_____

_____

_____

_____

_____

SEPTEMBER 28

20___ _____

_____

_____

_____

_____

_____

20___ _____

_____

_____

_____

_____

_____

20___ _____

_____

_____

_____

_____

_____

SEPTEMBER 29

20___ _____

_____

_____

_____

_____

_____

20___ _____

_____

_____

_____

_____

_____

20___ _____

_____

_____

_____

_____

_____

SEPTEMBER 30

20___ _____

_____

_____

_____

_____

_____

20___ _____

_____

_____

_____

_____

_____

20___ _____

_____

_____

_____

_____

_____

OCTOBER 1

20____ _____

_____

_____

_____

_____

_____

20____ _____

_____

_____

_____

_____

_____

20____ _____

_____

_____

_____

_____

_____

OCTOBER 2

20___ _____

_____

_____

_____

_____

_____

20___ _____

_____

_____

_____

_____

_____

20___ _____

_____

_____

_____

_____

_____

OCTOBER 3

20___ _____
_____
_____
_____
_____
_____

20___ _____
_____
_____
_____
_____
_____

20___ _____
_____
_____
_____
_____
_____

OCTOBER 4

20___ _____

_____

_____

_____

_____

_____

20___ _____

_____

_____

_____

_____

_____

20___ _____

_____

_____

_____

_____

_____

OCTOBER 5

20___ _____

_____

_____

_____

_____

_____

20___ _____

_____

_____

_____

_____

_____

20___ _____

_____

_____

_____

_____

_____

OCTOBER 6

20___ _____

_____

_____

_____

_____

_____

20___ _____

_____

_____

_____

_____

_____

20___ _____

_____

_____

_____

_____

_____

OCTOBER 7

20___ _____

_____

_____

_____

_____

_____

20___ _____

_____

_____

_____

_____

_____

20___ _____

_____

_____

_____

_____

_____

OCTOBER 8

20___ _____

_____

_____

_____

_____

_____

20___ _____

_____

_____

_____

_____

_____

20___ _____

_____

_____

_____

_____

_____

OCTOBER 9

20___ _____

_____

_____

_____

_____

_____

20___ _____

_____

_____

_____

_____

_____

20___ _____

_____

_____

_____

_____

_____

OCTOBER 10

20___ _____

_____

_____

_____

_____

_____

20___ _____

_____

_____

_____

_____

_____

20___ _____

_____

_____

_____

_____

_____

OCTOBER 11

20___ _____

_____
_____
_____
_____
_____

20___ _____

_____
_____
_____
_____
_____

20___ _____

_____
_____
_____
_____
_____

OCTOBER 12

20___ _____

_____

_____

_____

_____

_____

20___ _____

_____

_____

_____

_____

_____

20___ _____

_____

_____

_____

_____

_____

OCTOBER 13

20___ _____

_____

_____

_____

_____

_____

20___ _____

_____

_____

_____

_____

_____

20___ _____

_____

_____

_____

_____

_____

OCTOBER 14

20___ _____

_____

_____

_____

_____

_____

20___ _____

_____

_____

_____

_____

_____

20___ _____

_____

_____

_____

_____

_____

OCTOBER 15

20___ _____

_____

_____

_____

_____

_____

20___ _____

_____

_____

_____

_____

_____

20___ _____

_____

_____

_____

_____

_____

OCTOBER 16

20___ _____

_____

_____

_____

_____

_____

20___ _____

_____

_____

_____

_____

_____

20___ _____

_____

_____

_____

_____

_____

OCTOBER 17

20___ _____

_____

_____

_____

_____

_____

20___ _____

_____

_____

_____

_____

_____

20___ _____

_____

_____

_____

_____

_____

OCTOBER 18

20___ _____

_____

_____

_____

_____

_____

20___ _____

_____

_____

_____

_____

_____

20___ _____

_____

_____

_____

_____

_____

OCTOBER 19

20___ _____

_____

_____

_____

_____

_____

20___ _____

_____

_____

_____

_____

_____

20___ _____

_____

_____

_____

_____

_____

OCTOBER 20

20___ _____

_____

_____

_____

_____

_____

20___ _____

_____

_____

_____

_____

_____

20___ _____

_____

_____

_____

_____

_____

OCTOBER 21

20___ _____

_____

_____

_____

_____

_____

20___ _____

_____

_____

_____

_____

_____

20___ _____

_____

_____

_____

_____

_____

OCTOBER 22

20___ _____

_____

_____

_____

_____

_____

20___ _____

_____

_____

_____

_____

_____

20___ _____

_____

_____

_____

_____

_____

OCTOBER 23

20___ _____

20___ _____

20___ _____

OCTOBER 24

20___ _____

_____

_____

_____

_____

_____

20___ _____

_____

_____

_____

_____

_____

20___ _____

_____

_____

_____

_____

_____

OCTOBER 25

20___ _____

_____

_____

_____

_____

_____

20___ _____

_____

_____

_____

_____

_____

20___ _____

_____

_____

_____

_____

_____

OCTOBER 26

20___ _____

_____

_____

_____

_____

_____

20___ _____

_____

_____

_____

_____

_____

20___ _____

_____

_____

_____

_____

_____

OCTOBER 27

20___ _____

_____

_____

_____

_____

_____

20___ _____

_____

_____

_____

_____

_____

20___ _____

_____

_____

_____

_____

_____

OCTOBER 28

20___ _____

_____

_____

_____

_____

_____

20___ _____

_____

_____

_____

_____

_____

20___ _____

_____

_____

_____

_____

_____

OCTOBER 29

20___ _____

_____

_____

_____

_____

_____

20___ _____

_____

_____

_____

_____

_____

20___ _____

_____

_____

_____

_____

_____

OCTOBER 30

20___ _____

_____

_____

_____

_____

_____

20___ _____

_____

_____

_____

_____

_____

20___ _____

_____

_____

_____

_____

_____

OCTOBER 31

20___ _____

_____

_____

_____

_____

_____

20___ _____

_____

_____

_____

_____

_____

20___ _____

_____

_____

_____

_____

_____

NOVEMBER 1

20___ _____

_____

_____

_____

_____

_____

20___ _____

_____

_____

_____

_____

_____

20___ _____

_____

_____

_____

_____

_____

NOVEMBER 2

20___ _____

_____

_____

_____

_____

_____

20___ _____

_____

_____

_____

_____

_____

20___ _____

_____

_____

_____

_____

_____

NOVEMBER 3

20___ _____

_____

_____

_____

_____

_____

20___ _____

_____

_____

_____

_____

_____

20___ _____

_____

_____

_____

_____

_____

NOVEMBER 4

20___ _____
_____
_____
_____
_____
_____

20___ _____
_____
_____
_____
_____
_____

20___ _____
_____
_____
_____
_____
_____

NOVEMBER 5

20___ _____

_____
_____
_____
_____
_____

20___ _____

_____
_____
_____
_____
_____

20___ _____

_____
_____
_____
_____
_____

NOVEMBER 6

20___ _____

_____

_____

_____

_____

_____

20___ _____

_____

_____

_____

_____

_____

20___ _____

_____

_____

_____

_____

_____

NOVEMBER 7

20___ _____

_____

_____

_____

_____

_____

20___ _____

_____

_____

_____

_____

_____

20___ _____

_____

_____

_____

_____

_____

NOVEMBER 8

20___ _____

_____

_____

_____

_____

_____

20___ _____

_____

_____

_____

_____

_____

20___ _____

_____

_____

_____

_____

_____

NOVEMBER 9

20____ _____

_____

_____

_____

_____

_____

20____ _____

_____

_____

_____

_____

_____

20____ _____

_____

_____

_____

_____

_____

NOVEMBER 10

20___ _____

_____

_____

_____

_____

_____

20___ _____

_____

_____

_____

_____

_____

20___ _____

_____

_____

_____

_____

_____

NOVEMBER 11

20___ _____

_____

_____

_____

_____

_____

20___ _____

_____

_____

_____

_____

_____

20___ _____

_____

_____

_____

_____

_____

NOVEMBER 12

20___ _____
_____
_____
_____
_____
_____

20___ _____
_____
_____
_____
_____
_____

20___ _____
_____
_____
_____
_____
_____

NOVEMBER 13

20___ _____
_____
_____
_____
_____
_____

20___ _____
_____
_____
_____
_____
_____

20___ _____
_____
_____
_____
_____
_____

NOVEMBER 14

20___ _____

_____

_____

_____

_____

_____

20___ _____

_____

_____

_____

_____

_____

20___ _____

_____

_____

_____

_____

_____

NOVEMBER 15

20___ _____

_____

_____

_____

_____

_____

20___ _____

_____

_____

_____

_____

_____

20___ _____

_____

_____

_____

_____

_____

NOVEMBER 16

20___ _____

_____

_____

_____

_____

_____

20___ _____

_____

_____

_____

_____

_____

20___ _____

_____

_____

_____

_____

_____

NOVEMBER 17

20___ _____

_____

_____

_____

_____

_____

20___ _____

_____

_____

_____

_____

_____

20___ _____

_____

_____

_____

_____

_____

NOVEMBER 18

20___ _____
_____
_____
_____
_____
_____

20___ _____
_____
_____
_____
_____
_____

20___ _____
_____
_____
_____
_____
_____

NOVEMBER 19

20___ _____
_____
_____
_____
_____
_____

20___ _____
_____
_____
_____
_____
_____

20___ _____
_____
_____
_____
_____
_____

NOVEMBER 20

20___ _____

_____

_____

_____

_____

_____

20___ _____

_____

_____

_____

_____

_____

20___ _____

_____

_____

_____

_____

_____

NOVEMBER 21

20___ _____

_____

_____

_____

_____

_____

20___ _____

_____

_____

_____

_____

_____

20___ _____

_____

_____

_____

_____

_____

NOVEMBER 22

20___ _____
_____
_____
_____
_____
_____

20___ _____
_____
_____
_____
_____
_____

20___ _____
_____
_____
_____
_____
_____

NOVEMBER 23

20___ _____

_____

_____

_____

_____

_____

20___ _____

_____

_____

_____

_____

_____

20___ _____

_____

_____

_____

_____

_____

NOVEMBER 24

20___ _____

_____

_____

_____

_____

_____

20___ _____

_____

_____

_____

_____

_____

20___ _____

_____

_____

_____

_____

_____

NOVEMBER 25

20___ _____
_____
_____
_____
_____
_____

20___ _____
_____
_____
_____
_____
_____

20___ _____
_____
_____
_____
_____
_____

NOVEMBER 26

20___ _____

_____

_____

_____

_____

_____

20___ _____

_____

_____

_____

_____

_____

20___ _____

_____

_____

_____

_____

_____

NOVEMBER 27

20___ _____

_____

_____

_____

_____

_____

20___ _____

_____

_____

_____

_____

_____

20___ _____

_____

_____

_____

_____

_____

NOVEMBER 28

20___ _____

_____

_____

_____

_____

_____

20___ _____

_____

_____

_____

_____

_____

20___ _____

_____

_____

_____

_____

_____

NOVEMBER 29

20___ _____

_____

_____

_____

_____

_____

20___ _____

_____

_____

_____

_____

_____

20___ _____

_____

_____

_____

_____

_____

NOVEMBER 30

20___ _____

_____

_____

_____

_____

_____

20___ _____

_____

_____

_____

_____

_____

20___ _____

_____

_____

_____

_____

_____

DECEMBER 1

20____ _____

_____

_____

_____

_____

_____

20____ _____

_____

_____

_____

_____

_____

20____ _____

_____

_____

_____

_____

_____

DECEMBER 2

20___ _____
_____
_____
_____
_____
_____

20___ _____
_____
_____
_____
_____
_____

20___ _____
_____
_____
_____
_____
_____

DECEMBER 3

20___ _____

_____

_____

_____

_____

_____

20___ _____

_____

_____

_____

_____

_____

20___ _____

_____

_____

_____

_____

_____

DECEMBER 4

20___ _____

_____

_____

_____

_____

_____

20___ _____

_____

_____

_____

_____

_____

20___ _____

_____

_____

_____

_____

_____

DECEMBER 5

20___ _____

_____

_____

_____

_____

_____

20___ _____

_____

_____

_____

_____

_____

20___ _____

_____

_____

_____

_____

_____

DECEMBER 6

20___ _____
_____
_____
_____
_____
_____

20___ _____
_____
_____
_____
_____
_____

20___ _____
_____
_____
_____
_____
_____

DECEMBER 7

20___ _____
_____
_____
_____
_____
_____

20___ _____
_____
_____
_____
_____
_____

20___ _____
_____
_____
_____
_____
_____

DECEMBER 8

20___ _____

_____

_____

_____

_____

_____

20___ _____

_____

_____

_____

_____

_____

20___ _____

_____

_____

_____

_____

_____

DECEMBER 9

20___ _____

_____

_____

_____

_____

_____

20___ _____

_____

_____

_____

_____

_____

20___ _____

_____

_____

_____

_____

_____

DECEMBER 10

20___ _____

_____

_____

_____

_____

_____

20___ _____

_____

_____

_____

_____

_____

20___ _____

_____

_____

_____

_____

_____

DECEMBER 11

20___ _____

_____

_____

_____

_____

_____

20___ _____

_____

_____

_____

_____

_____

20___ _____

_____

_____

_____

_____

_____

DECEMBER 12

20___ _____

_____

_____

_____

_____

_____

20___ _____

_____

_____

_____

_____

_____

20___ _____

_____

_____

_____

_____

_____

DECEMBER 13

20___ _____

_____

_____

_____

_____

_____

20___ _____

_____

_____

_____

_____

_____

20___ _____

_____

_____

_____

_____

_____

DECEMBER 14

20___ _____

_____

_____

_____

_____

_____

20___ _____

_____

_____

_____

_____

_____

20___ _____

_____

_____

_____

_____

_____

DECEMBER 15

20___ _____

_____

_____

_____

_____

_____

20___ _____

_____

_____

_____

_____

20___ _____

_____

_____

_____

_____

_____

DECEMBER 16

20___ _____

_____

_____

_____

_____

_____

20___ _____

_____

_____

_____

_____

_____

20___ _____

_____

_____

_____

_____

_____

DECEMBER 17

20___ _____

_____

_____

_____

_____

_____

20___ _____

_____

_____

_____

_____

_____

20___ _____

_____

_____

_____

_____

_____

DECEMBER 18

20___ _____

_____

_____

_____

_____

_____

20___ _____

_____

_____

_____

_____

_____

20___ _____

_____

_____

_____

_____

_____

DECEMBER 19

20___ _____
_____
_____
_____
_____
_____

20___ _____
_____
_____
_____
_____
_____

20___ _____
_____
_____
_____
_____
_____

DECEMBER 20

20___ _____

_____

_____

_____

_____

_____

20___ _____

_____

_____

_____

_____

_____

20___ _____

_____

_____

_____

_____

_____

DECEMBER 21

20___ _____

_____

_____

_____

_____

_____

20___ _____

_____

_____

_____

_____

_____

20___ _____

_____

_____

_____

_____

_____

DECEMBER 22

20___ _____

_____

_____

_____

_____

_____

20___ _____

_____

_____

_____

_____

_____

20___ _____

_____

_____

_____

_____

_____

DECEMBER 23

20___ _____

_____

_____

_____

_____

_____

20___ _____

_____

_____

_____

_____

_____

20___ _____

_____

_____

_____

_____

_____

DECEMBER 24

20___ _____

_____

_____

_____

_____

_____

20___ _____

_____

_____

_____

_____

_____

20___ _____

_____

_____

_____

_____

_____

DECEMBER 25

20___ _____
_____
_____
_____
_____
_____

20___ _____
_____
_____
_____
_____
_____

20___ _____
_____
_____
_____
_____
_____

DECEMBER 26

20___ _____

_____

_____

_____

_____

_____

20___ _____

_____

_____

_____

_____

_____

20___ _____

_____

_____

_____

_____

_____

DECEMBER 27

20___ _____

_____
_____
_____
_____
_____

20___ _____

_____
_____
_____
_____
_____

20___ _____

_____
_____
_____
_____
_____

DECEMBER 28

20___ _____

_____

_____

_____

_____

_____

20___ _____

_____

_____

_____

_____

_____

20___ _____

_____

_____

_____

_____

_____

DECEMBER 29

20____ _____

20____ _____

20____ _____

DECEMBER 30

20___ _____
_____
_____
_____
_____
_____

20___ _____
_____
_____
_____
_____
_____

20___ _____
_____
_____
_____
_____
_____

DECEMBER 31

20___ _____

_____

_____

_____

_____

_____

20___ _____

_____

_____

_____

_____

_____

20___ _____

_____

_____

_____

_____

_____

Eternally grateful for...

_____
_____
_____
_____
_____
_____
_____
_____
_____
_____
_____
_____
_____
_____
_____
_____
_____
_____
_____